WIPING STARS
FROM YOUR
SLEEVES

WIPING STARS
FROM YOUR
SLEEVES

POEMS BY DAVID JAMES

SHANTI ARTS PUBLISHING
BRUNSWICK, MAINE

WIPING STARS FROM YOUR SLEEVES

Published by Shanti Arts Publishing
Interior and cover design by Shanti Arts Designs

Cover image: Greg Rakozy on unsplash.com

Shanti Arts LLC
193 Hillside Road
Brunswick, Maine 04011

shantiarts.com

Printed in the United States of America

ISBN: 978-1-951651-97-8 (softcover)

Library of Congress Control Number: 2021946017

WIPING STARS
FROM YOUR
SLEEVES

POEMS BY DAVID JAMES

SHANTI ARTS PUBLISHING

BRUNSWICK, MAINE

Published by Shanti Arts Publishing
Interior and cover design by Shanti Arts Designs

Cover image: Greg Rakozy on unsplash.com

Shanti Arts LLC
193 Hillside Road
Brunswick, Maine 04011

shantiarts.com

Printed in the United States of America

ISBN: 978-1-951651-97-8 (softcover)

Library of Congress Control Number: 2021946017

This book is dedicated to one of the Wild Wooly
Women of the West, the love of my life and
partner in this crazy journey, Debra Marie.

CONTENTS

ACROSS THE GREAT OCEAN

ACKNOWLEDGEMENTS

Bryant Literary Review: "Out of the Limelight"

Chiron Review: "Endgame"

Escape into Life: "It Starts with G, Like God," "A Thin Space," and "What We Do for Love"

Evening Street Journal: "Ars Poetica: Kroger's on Grand River"

A Gathering of Tribes: "Dear Poem"

GNU Journal: "Back to Basics"

Mizmor Anthology: "My Sacred Scroll"

Peacock Journal: "Interview with Buddha"

Peninsula Poets: "Seven, Eleven, Not."

Poetry Leaves: "Back in the Day"

PPP Ezine: "Fall of the Party Girl"

Talking River Review: "Walking Down the Mountain"

Third Wednesday: "Recipe for Hope"

Uppagus: "The Ultimate Consequence"

Voices de la Luna Earth: "A Loop Head Blessing"

With eternal thanks to Thomas Lynch for the use of his cottage on the Loop Head in Ireland where many of these poems were written.

With admiration to all of the Irish poets (and people) who inspire me (those mentioned in this book and those not).

With appreciation to Oakland Community College for granting me a sabbatical in 2018–19, allowing the time to read and write.

With love to my mom, Sharon, who started it all. And a special thanks to my lovely children who have given me six glorious and beautiful grandchildren.

OUR LONG SHORE

We are born of a nation, and
we are shaped by its features.
—Tracy K. Smith

IT'S JUST WHAT YOU DO IF GIVEN THE CHANCE

—for Marc Sheehan

I woke up this morning
on the wrong side of history.
So I did what I've always dreamed of doing:
I invented myself and a world
complete with the things I loved and liked and wanted.

I made myself so happy and grateful
that I couldn't stop smiling.
I took a deep breath and dealt out good fortune
like playing cards to my kids and grands, family and friends.

With the wink of an eye, I gave every person
on the face of the earth food and water,
a home and a job that used their individual talents,
that gave them a real sense of purpose.

I bestowed freedom and equality
between all genders and races and religions
by flicking my little finger, and I baked
respect and tolerance into everyone's DNA.

Then I leaned back and dissolved every map line
on the globe, created one big-ass country.
By flaring my left nostril, the wars dried up,
all hate dried up, every vendetta became a colored bow
placed on a gift given to children
for no reason other than kindness.

Maybe I was just dreaming,
but if this was the wrong side of history,
I don't want to be right.

WALKING DOWN THE MOUNTAIN

it's a little strange
at my age to think about how many years

i have left to break bread with family and friends,
to wrestle with grandkids or even play golf. i can't change

the facts—in sixteen years, i'll be eighty,
and most men don't live that long. my career

as a human being is coming to an end. it's not that i worry
about it or spend hours each day moping around,

sullen and upset. it's just there, always there, in clear
view near the back of my brain where it blends

in with whatever i make for breakfast and morning coffee.
maybe this is how wisdom arrives—like scrooge,

the future is suddenly in my line of sight and i realize
what really matters, what's important. so i roll up my sleeves

and hold each moment a little longer, blessed to still be around.

KISS ME

Chance that an American aged 18–24 has never kissed anyone: 1 in 5.
—"Index," *Harper's*, October 2018

It seems hard to believe
these days
that twenty percent under the age of twenty-four
haven't been kissed.

Think of all the ways
there are to meet people, hook-up or more:
Fling, Naughty, Snapsext, Tinder.
Technology has opened the lock
to everyone's bedroom.
There's no benefit to acting demur
and coy, or trying to block
your online profile. Life is short
and the prospects are many.
You have to kiss a lot of frogs,
remove dozens of warts,
sort through buckets of pennies,
before you find your soul mate.

So, put on your fancy clothes,
pucker those lips and start kissing. Think of the heart
as your home, your mouth as the front gate.

THE RED BOX

Sabrina carried a red box, smaller than a shoe box, everywhere she went. It was with her at the grocery store, nestled in her shopping cart; at work in her desk; at the cross-country meet in her lap. "What's in the box?" Josh asked. "Oh, nothing," she replied. She had a purse so we ruled out her wallet or keys. When we pressed her on the subject, she never gave us hints and usually ended up saying, "It's none of your damn business."

Josh thought it was an extra pair of dentures; Cody suggested a gun, small caliber. Paul said it might be love notes from her youthful days. Mitchell was sure it was duct tape and pepper spray. When we asked any of Sabrina's female friends they said they didn't know either, but we never believed them. Women stick together on things like this.

We created elaborate plans to steal the red box and look inside but we failed on every occasion due to miscues or deceit, faulty assumptions or treacherous acts. Mostly, it was pure incompetence on our part.

In the end, we joined in and got our own red boxes. Like the Red Hat Society, we were easily recognizable wherever we went. No one ever said what they carried in their boxes, but we assumed birth certificates, savings bonds, liquid nails, phone chargers, eyeglass repair kits, Canadian money, seeds. Most of my friends assumed I had pocket knives and marijuana, but there were dead wrong.

In my red box, invisible to everyone except me, I carried my dreams.

AFTER FORTY-ONE   YEARS

—after Dennis Hinrichsen

I bang love against
memory and you bang memory
against truth.
I bang truth against
routine and you bang routine
against my face
with more wrinkles and forehead
than necessary//I bang routine against
your sleeping body on the couch/
as the TV's glow
dances across your eyelids.

and when we bang love against
time/it breaks/crumbles/
scatters on the floor.
We sweep up the mess and place it
in a flower pot on the counter.
You plant a seed while I get water.

Then I bang love against
hope and you bang hope
against my heart.
But when I bang my heart against
your heart/blood goes everywhere—
on our hands/faces/on our shirts.
With a red finger/
you draw my name on the wall.
So I bang my lips against
your lips and draw
your body into my body.

A single green stem
rises out of the flower pot/
blooming into something
beautiful/
something we'll never be able
to know or name.

DEAR POEM

—for Eric Torgersen

I want you to reach inside my chest, grab my heart
and squeeze it
until it shouts
so loudly, people turn to stare at me. I want you to dive
from the top ledge of my brain, somersaulting into the blue sea below
while Mozart
plays piano
and a million ballerinas dance and twirl under the crashing waves.

I want you to look me straight in the eyes and whisper the words
even a scarecrow
could believe.
I want you to lie to me in a calm voice and send me on a wild ride
through the heavens and forests, through the core of the earth,
into the third
ring of Saturn
until every known fact becomes a unique and colorful feather.

BACK TO BASICS

pull off
the first layer of skin
and expose the bone
  cut a fine slice
down your chest
to remove the heart
  open the forehead
and pick out the brain debris
left there from
childhood

lower yourself down
on a flimsy rope
into the middle of your past
and take photos
of cave paintings fingered in blood
  the crude stick-like drawings
of fears and doubts   a missed chance here
a chance loss there
all captured on the wall
of some earlier life

this is archeology and anthropology
this is psychic-dissection
  personal surgery without anesthesia
                the mining for
your creation story
in a country
you've only dreamed about

THE ULTIMATE CONSEQUENCE

Every trap I set was empty, not even one snapped shut. These were clever chipmunks. No matter what I used—peanut butter, pistachios, almonds, walnuts, cashews—each small rodent trap, and I had forty-six of them, would be empty by morning. Every other week, I'd catch a helpless sparrow in one, maybe a stray mouse. The chipmunks, however, were taking over. At last count, I had tallied one hundred and seven, though it did cross my mind that I was being scammed: maybe there were five or six who ran back and forth, in full view, to give the impression that there were more. Maybe my neighbor, Roger, whom I despised, had hired this criminal band of chipmunks to desecrate my home, dig their burrows under my foundation until my basement began leaking water, causing huge financial repairs. Maybe Roger taught them how to remove the nuts carefully, to enjoy the fruits of their devious labor, to watch my face as I walked around, swearing at each open trap, replacing the lost nuts. Or maybe Roger was a chipmunk himself simply disguised as a human. Maybe he was the father of this band of juvenile delinquents, the mastermind of my sorrow.

Roger had planned to make my life insufferable so I'd sell my house and he would buy it because he always envied my built-in pool.

It seemed like a perfect plan until I realized my only hope was to kill Roger.

SEVEN, ELEVEN, NOT.

I'm not a lucky guy.
Take me to any casino
and I'll lose
$200 in ten minutes flat.
Sweepstakes, horse racing,
sports betting, poker, the lottery—
they suck
the money out of my wallet
faster and easier than grandkids.

If there's a pothole in the road,
I'll hit it.
If there's a defective TV,
I'll buy it.
My mail gets lost at least 50%
of the time.
I've even forgotten the names
of my two younger brothers.

Balding, with bad knees and failing eyesight,
I'm the one who backs the car
into the lamppost,
who loses his credit card in Canada,
who splits his pants kneeling for communion,
        the guy who gets butt-dialed from heaven
and is only able to hear angels singing
in the background while God
falls asleep on his throne,
snoring into eternity.

MY SACRED SCROLL

among our fragile, vanishing gifts
—Keith Taylor, "Acolytes in the Bird-while"

my list is too long

to write down,
my blessings piled high in crates and boxes

that will never be strong
enough to hold.

they come and go, are lost and found,
blowing in and out of reach:

a sweet smile, a call from an old friend,
a lone cucumber, the sound

of your voice shining like gold,
walking a sandy beach

with grandkids, dodging waves
and laughing. I try my best

to keep these moments, to carve each
memory on some sacred scroll

in my brain, to catalogue and save
them all for the dark times

yet to come, but I can't. they kiss
my forehead and are gone, like these days

washing over my grateful soul.

WHATEVER YOU DO

don't imagine yourself on a dirt road

driving 70 m.p.h. at night
with a quarter moon stuck in the highest branch
of a small birch.
and don't imagine there's a well-dressed toad
in the front seat lighting another joint,
your third, which, once smoked, will bring an avalanche
of memories, an earthquake of hurt
back into view: how you forgot about the dynamite
in the trunk, how you tried to anoint
the crossing guard on Broad Street with tears as St. Togglehorse.

don't imagine yourself lost in the desert.

don't imagine the carnage at the campsite
where you found love at first glance
and signed up for a crash course
in heartbreak. don't imagine those pills you took
forced you to steer the car into the ditch. in hindsight,
you should have walked home and danced
in your misery. so don't imagine yourself pinned and hurt
in a flaming car, trying to shake out what can't be shook.

FALL OF THE PARTY GIRL

Fall arrives with a pony keg and six fifths
of Kentucky bourbon,
her face painted orange, yellow and red.
She screams into the cool sky
ready to party into a myth
and vanish after the first snowfall.

Someone said
she'd try any drug, sleep with any guy,
spend the night in a garbage bin.
And that's not all:
she has Daddy issues.
The old man didn't hug her enough; didn't look her in the eye;
never took her by the chin
and said she was beautiful with those baby blues
and long hair.   So, today,
if you pay her any attention,
she'll jump your bones, ravage your bed,
tear you to pieces and leave without saying goodbye.

When you get up, look out the window: it'll be cold, white and gray.

A QUESTION OF FAITH

—for Pope Francis

I'm at my aunt's funeral, who died
too soon, and it's in a massive Catholic church,
St. Robert's, a saint I can't recall in the Bible.

It's a beautiful and sad service with readings
about God's love, the resurrection, suffering, forgiveness
and hope, how life is a gift that collides

with death, how much we don't understand as humans.
And then the priest, before communion, tells the gathering
that only "practicing Catholics" are allowed to partake

in Christ's body and blood, a sacrament meant to bless
believers with God's ultimate sacrifice. And I think,
what about lapsed Catholics or former Catholics?

What about non-practicing Catholics? Wanna-be Catholics?
What happens to those protestants who go up, break
the bread and drink the wine? Are they captured, burned

at the stake? Are there dungeons below
the sacristy? The dissonance between God's word
and the church's practice hits me like a brick:

if Jesus himself stumbled up the aisle,
bloody and lost, hell, he'd be turned away.

A GOOD PART

I spend a good part of my day
watching leaves
commit suicide, jumping off branches
thirty, forty, even sixty feet up under a gray
sky.

There's a good part of my belief
system that tries to understand
what fall
should mean to me as a sixty-three
year old white male
born to privilege, a sturdy spoon in my hand,
to good parents who loved me
and did their best.

The trees shake and undress, take their stand
against winter who stops by
for three or four months to see
how much snow and cold I can take.
The allusions are obvious: I need
to let go; change will come; tomorrow's freeze
can slow the world to a snail's
pace. Nothing I do or say can make
the fall longer, the winter shorter.

Nothing can slow down the hands
of any clock, for me or anyone's sake.

I spend a good part of my life wondering why.

INTERVIEW WITH BUDDHA

Like Christ, I was in my thirties before
I could see through the fog and understand
a thing or two. With time and experience, I found wisdom
in the sunlit trees, in the rushing streams, in the hum
of bees dancing on the Musk Rose. My holy land
was the here and now, the moment, the dirt floor

on which I slept.   Since living is pain,
and wanting brings despair, the key is to release
all desire, unclench your sweaty fists, and allow karma
to fall on you like a warm rain, slow to thaw
your frozen heart. As you let go, the world breathes
in your face: enlightened, there's nothing to lose. Or gain.

BACK IN THE DAY

A couple billion years ago, I was a freckle-faced kid
with a baseball cap, a glove and a bike

to ride to the fields at North Shore Elementary,
which is where I lived after breakfast until dinner.
A billion years later, I was smitten and took to you like

clouds take to the sky. You were the lock, me, the key,
and we opened each other's secrets.

And then a half billion years ago,
the babies came and crawled across the land,
rearranging our house and sleep schedule, breaking the tea set,

finally rising up on two feet to demand full control
of our lives. It's been several million years now

and the grandkids carry our hearts around
on silver platters while the sun and stars shine down,
refusing to let on why or even how.

A GOOD LOOK IN THE MIRROR

You can walk down the long dirt road
with your head up your ass.

>You can ignore every sign sent to you
>and pretend you know the answer.
>You can piss into the wind, live in a glass
>house, kiss every ugly toad
>you can get your slimy hands on.
>You can cheat your lovers and friends,
>ruin every family holiday, steal
>from your employer and neighbors.
>In fact, you can spend
>a lifetime treating people like morons,
>focusing only on your personal needs,
>being brutally selfish to the core.
>No one will stop you. Life will go on—
>the snows will come and go, spring will find
>her place and lobby for more
>tulips and daffodils, less weeds.
>You see, your life doesn't add up to anything
>unless you do the math. You can divide
>or multiply, add or subtract. You can be a fraction
>of your potential or work toward being whole.

Nothing says you need happiness or love on your side.
One cardinal is killed by a hawk; another rises and sings.

I WANDER AND YOU WANDER

—for Tracie Little

A man who wanders from the way of understanding
will rest in the assembly of the dead.

—Proverbs 21

we all spend time
in the assembly of the dead
because everyone strays
everyone gets lost
everyone picks the short end of the stick
and believes he's invincible
invisible
incapable of being caught

everyone jumps and comes up short
falls in the water   or   off the edge of a cliff
we misjudge   misinterpret
we see what we want
and not the truth
standing before us
shouting our name into the night sky
and then reading off
a long list of mistakes made
of words said
of lies and blunders and deceptions
and thin slices of red meat cut out of our hearts
when we hungered
for more than we deserved

that's when
the dead assemble around, chanting nothing
out of their decaying mouths
clapping wildly as fingers and hands crumble to their feet
reminding us that any breath
      is sacred
that all ground
      is holy

I'LL KEEP YOU RIGHT HERE

Who needs the whole girl if you've got her knee?
Joseph Brodsky, "I Sit by the Window"

I keep some bone dust

of my father in a tiny urn in the dining room.
I have one grandma's tooth, another grandma's rib,
two hairs from my maternal grandpa and the left trigger finger
from the other. It's stuck in a planter like it could bloom.
Not sure what my kids will keep of me, but I trust
it'll bring back only good memories:
playing ball, laughing at hide-and-seek, swimming in the lake.
And if you go down before me, love, which I doubt,
I'll keep your heart in a shiny red box
locked away so it won't break.

As in life, I'll hold you close and throw away the key.

HOW TO FIND LOVE IN THE MIDDLE
OF ALL THIS CRAZINESS

—for Stu Dybek

"So what do you want to grow here?" The question came from Rose, a young woman I had fallen in love with years before I had the chance to touch her eyelids with my fingertips. She had beautiful eyelids.

"How about lawn tractors?" I said. "We could sell them and buy a tree fort down by the lake." I said this even though I knew Rose was afraid of sharp blades and afraid of trees. You might say it was a test of her love for me.

Rose looked up to check the status of the clouds, her white hair short on one side, long on the other; one blue eye, one hazel. She squinted a bit before spitting in my direction. She missed.

I knew it wasn't fair of me. But life's not fair. And love is always cruel. I had spent the whole summer loving Rose and I wasn't going to be hurt again the way I was with Melody, or Jenny, or Carrie, Gabby, Kim, Hannah, and especially, Mrs. Bedletter. That last one was a gerbil.

"Do you think the soil is good enough for tractors?" Rose asked, looking back up to the sky. It was a smart, tactical response, one void of any commitment. She was stalling for a change of heart.

"It's fine," I said, nailing it. Now I'd find out for sure if she was the one.

Rose coughed, looked at me, winked her blue eye twice and licked her lips. Those lips reminded me of two earthworms on a rainy day on the sidewalk of someone's face.

"If you think it'll work, then I'm all in," she said.

That's when I swore there was the smell of cut grass in the air, birds carrying gallons of gasoline, spark plugs barking in the distance.

AFTER YEARS OF BEHAVIORIAL THERAPY

the world comes to me
when I call it
circling my feet
purring and looking up

whatever I work for   happens
whatever I believe   comes true
whatever I am   is what I should be
and nothing less

whether it rains or snows or shines down outside
I wake up and jump out of bed
knowing the day is mine
to twist or turn or bend as I see fit

this gift
pure and simple
is given to each of us

whether we accept it
or not
is the only
difference

WHAT WE DO FOR LOVE

—for Aunt Jackie and Uncle Don

January 4th
and it's 51 degrees, sunny, no snow. It's Michigan, for God's sake,
the middle of winter. I made dinner tonight—broiled Mahi-Mahi

with brown sugared
carrots, artichoke and Parmesan bites. It's love. You'll burn at the stake,
stand in front of a firing squad, or swim to the bottom of the sea

to find the lost ring thrown
from the ship's rear deck when you love someone. Like
my uncle who's caring for my dying aunt and would buy the moon,

pay any cost
if it would make her better, let her sit up and stare out back at the sun
on the bird bath, on that small deer wandering through their yard.

But sometimes, nothing helps, not even love,
and all you can do is be there in the room, placing a damp cloth
on her forehead, squeezing her hand just a little too hard.

OUT OF THE LIMELIGHT

Maybe it's my dislike for coconut,
my aversion to horror movies.

It could be because I teach
at a community college, not
some high-powered ivy league school.

Could it be that I've never used "synergy"
in a poem before?

In a weak moment, I wonder why
most of the world ignores me
and my work, but then I realize it's pure conceit

asking that question. Instead, I'll explore
the aisles of everyday living.

I'll turn a cold shoulder to endowed chairs;
hell, I have no interest in a seashore
bungalow on Cape Cod, or being asked to testify

before Congress on how to bring
the classics to rural second-graders.

Let me have my quiet life, dinner with the grandkids,
golf with my wife, nothing to do in the evening
except write a poem or two in my underwear.

RECIPE FOR HOPE

—for Jack Ridl

turn off the computer
and cell phone
close your eyes
and picture the smile
of your very first love

eat seven cookies
and one piece of fruit
along with a bowl
of your favorite cereal
sprinkled with either
cinnamon
or chocolate chips

walk one mile
in any direction
then walk back

draw this picture
a large tree with cars and fish
attached as leaves
and a sun above wrapped
as a present
in the sky

and then sit in any room
for 59 minutes
imagining what your
life would be like
if every wish
you ever had
came true

ENDGAME

The woman lets her hair fall out,

gathers and weaves it into yarn
for slippers or hats.
No one notices that her bald head
looks like an egg, cracked. The terrible drought
came that same year,
the year we lost the house and the cat.
The house we could explain, but a cat spread
like a pancake on the street had no charm.
With two spatulas, I scraped up the smear
and buried what was left. But that's how I want to go—

struck down while making banana bread,
or golfing, swimming, walking out back on the farm.
Keep me away from beds with intravenous tubes, lying flat
on my ass, the eerie drizzle of an oboe
in the background. Instead, I'll lose my hair
and weave it into baby mittens. I'll pull the fire alarm
and blame it on a ghost. I'll wrestle a wombat
in a fair fight. Let the big one knock me dead,

quick and sure, with none of this shit, gasping for air.

BEFORE THE END OF NOVEMBER, WINTER ARRIVES

The snow falls like salt
on a world of mashed potatoes.

It's Thursday and Deb is working late while her sister,
Cheryl, lies in bed upstairs,
doctor's orders, for forty-eight hours.
It's her back, and no one's fault

other than heredity and genes.
We're all dealt a different hand

and play the cards the best we can.
Some hit the jackpot early; some cower
on the ledge of a tenth floor apartment.
Some hold their cards close

to their chests, stay inside and wait
for the world to find them; others plan

a victory parade with their beautiful straight flushes.
The days come and go, but winter stays.
The hawk in our backyard tree hopes
for a squirrel or rabbit, a dove, some delicious bait

to show itself. If he plays his cards right, who knows?
He may sleep tonight on a full stomach.

ARS POETICA: KROGER'S ON GRAND RIVER

—for Chloe Maple

I take my granddaughter to the grocery store
to buy dinner; she chooses a chocolate smoothie,
Brie cheese and sea salt pita chips, refusing
the cold shrimp with dipping sauce,
the sushi, the fried chicken.

In the car, parked under a streetlight,
we share chunks of soft cheese with chips
and talk about the day, but mostly
about how good the cheese tastes.

I'm not sure her parents would approve
of this dinner,
but I'm a ji-chan and it's my job
to give her a taste of freedom and choice,
within reason, of course.
The joy in her face and voice
is enough to make my heart smile.

And you never know:
this may be her memory of me,
decades from now,
when she walks into a grocery store
to buy something
to eat
with her own granddaughter.

THE WORLD'S RADAR

We're on the downhill slide, friends,
as our teeth yellow and chip,
as the pill bottles line up in the cupboards.
This damn knee gives out at least
once a week. My left hip
can predict rain—a steady downpour
or a light sprinkle. I find myself spent
before any money's been thrown on the table.
I remember the tune but forget the chords.

                              In the end,
we have to lighten up and loosen our grip,
take smaller bites, chew longer. There's something
to be said about a good smoothie blend.
The world's radar keeps moving and there we are, a blip
on the big screen, a flash of light, then nothing more.

LET THE WORLD GO

—for Josh Hoover

There's more to life than increasing its speed.
—Gandhi

The knots in my stomach
tell the whole truth:
    untie me, Lord.
    Take away the phone, the computer,
collapse Facebook into the dust
of the Ethernet.
    Lift every worry and stress, every pain and obligation
off my back,   drown each disappointment
and failed dream in the Great Sea of the Past.
    Untie the fear of the day
from around my neck
and let me sit here in the moment, in the backyard
under an apple tree, listening to birds, a dog barking,
the neighbor's lawnmower.
    Let my mind stay put, hunkered down
and content to be alone.
    Let the world go on without me for a while.
    Let the future fall asleep in the grass and dream
of settling down with a wife and kids, a modest vegetable garden
at the side of the house.
              I want each minute to last a month,
          each day, a year or two.
    Untie me, Lord,
and I'll have the strength to kneel before you,
to find heaven in the smiles of my grandchildren,
to wallow in the blessings
rising up like roses
at my fingertips.

ACROSS THE GREAT OCEAN

*Imitation is not just the sincerest form of
flattery—it's the sincerest form of learning.*

—George Bernard Shaw

IN THE GREAT BOOK OF DREAMS

The days we despair of each other...
—Harry Clifton, "Where We Live"

Let's assume you were never born.
You were an idea, a possibility,
a wish for a short period of time,
but a missed chance
in the end.
Those brown eyes, that smile,
the long red hair drifted into a forgotten dream.

You never saw your mother crying,
your father slamming the door
on his path to a twelve-year drinking binge.
It was better this way,
less heartbreak, no physical pain,
spared the despair
that follows the living.

Let's assume you could see
everything you lost, tally up
all the hurtful words and sayings,
every slap to the face, every dream
crushed by indifference or bad luck.

You would thank
your would-be parents, now long dead.
You and your absent siblings
would sit around a table,
remembering all you never did,
raising an empty glass
to nothing,
to no one.

AROUND EVERY CORNER

Between my finger and my thumb
My squat pen rests.

—Seamus Heaney, "Digging"

And what will
come of it when I dig is anyone's guess,

especially mine. Every decent writer is at a loss for words
when asked why and how. He stares out at a crow and three horses
and then writes about a man with six mannequins he dresses
up before he drills
every night
with punches and kicks, slams and shouts. Why? Why not?

The fields become memories; the waves, voices from beyond.
Love is a cliff edge; a hole in the ground, dark wings.
Storm clouds sailing in from the sea are knots
that might
untie a heart
and beg it to feel again. All things crumble into sand,
get buried or swept away in the wind. Even your eyes, love,
are torches, beacons of light guiding me into safe harbor.

The rain pours down, drumming the ship's deck,
so I lift the pen in my hand
and start.

IF IT TAKES THIS MUCH WORK

They say love hangs on for dear life . . .
Sara Berkeley, "Glaces, Sorbets"

By the raw skin of my fingertips,
I dangle off the cliff
of love,
legs kicking,
praying for a great wave of wind to lift
me up enough to slip

back up onto ground. Ah, what romantic
bullshit...
If your love hangs on for dear life, it's the wrong
kind of love.
That's sabotage
or terrorism; that's when the insecure and strong
beat down the will of another and slit

their heart.   No, love doesn't hang on—
it hugs, it grows, it laughs, it opens its arms
wide enough to carry
all your dreams
and fears. With your feet on the ground, firm
and sure, love walks the shoreline with you, admiring the swans.

ON THE THIRD DAY

Where do they put all the breasts
they cut off anyhow?

Clairr O'Connor, "Listening to Cindy"

Probably the same place
they throw the bits of skin

      from millions of circumcisions,
          or the pounds of cellulose

sliced from waists and bellies.
Probably where they toss the ribbons

      of flesh after face lifts,
        after nose jobs and eye reconstruction.

They probably drop them in the same bin
they deposit kidneys and appendix,

      feet and legs, moles and bits
      of skin cancer. Somewhere in the world,

all the human parts cut off—the breasts and chins and fingers—
mix together in a huge vat of misfits,

      churning for that day they'll rise up
        whole again.

AMBER ALERT

—for Jim Daniels

> *. . . the sound of paper*
> *screaming in the hand.*
> —Patrick Galvin, "Nothing is Safe"

I wrote a poem one night

and by morning, it was gone,
a run-away. It left a note
full of spelling and punctuation errors,
which was part of the con,
I think, especially when it wrote,
"Ive lift to pee fee
vers." Hell, it *was* free verse.

I called the missing poems department
and reported: *"short poem with acne*
wearing a hoodie, blue jeans, and a terse
final line bordering on being humorous.
Last seen going to bed."

Of course, the officials claimed this happens
every day, young poems going for bust,
refusing to be published and read,
refusing to be caught between the covers.
They want a life of their own without rhyme and meter,
without meaning and purpose, one of those boring ass lives

where each word leaves nothing to be discovered.

A QUESTION OF LEGACY

> *Which lasts longer, poetry or drink?*
> —David Wheatley, "Sonnets to James Clarence Morgan"

Easy question: poetry, which may be why
I write verse. I like to think
my words will travel beyond the day of my demise,
which, considering that prospect, may be why I drink.

PREDICTING NOTHING

The day is pulling away from me,
gathering into itself . . .
—Eileen Sheehan, "Thoughts Procured by Twilight"

You can say what you want

about the weather here,
I won't believe it. I've lived it now for a month:
a mist in the morning, gray sky; by noon, it rains with the wind
picking up; in an hour, white clouds appear
and it's sunny; a dark front
from the east moves in, partly cloudy; it rains, turns to mist
before the sun bursts out into a blue sky.

The cows graze, the sheep graze and neither thinks
about the rain or sun or clouds.
They wander in the fields, chewing, oblivious as to why
the flies are gone. If thousands of fish
fell down from above, they wouldn't bat
an eye or raise a hoof.

Maybe that's how we should be: just go on
with life whether it rains or snows, whether we lose
a job or earn a promotion, win the lottery or fall off a roof:

keep our heads down, wander and chew,
                              ignore the flies and gnats.

MAKING A CASE FOR RECLAMATION

After the murder, I called a meeting
to see if we were happy.
—Matthew Sweeney, "Gold"

But no one in the group showed. They took
the money and vanished, blood on their hands,
paint on their faces,
salt in their hair.
I called the meeting to order and I was the only one present, no band,
no ribbons, no champagne, nothing cooked.

Though I wasn't happy, apparently, everyone else was.
On their boats, at the resorts, in the casinos,
my colleagues
were oblivious
to my reservations, which I listed on poster paper in two rows
with green magic marker. It's what one does

when one's conscience is compromised and guilt
drips down into the bottom of one's heart.
We killed
the wrong guy,
so now I have to hunt down my friends and kill them to start
the case for redemption. I have to turn a boulder into silt,

a pigeon into a deer, a mistake into a virtue.
After the murder, I realized the only holy path
to salvation
was to confess
or redress the deed. I totaled up the sins, did the math
and made sure those involved were erased. It's the least I could do.

YIN / YANG

And a man on the road
is singing for no reason.
—Michael Coady, "Though There are Torturers"

Even though our president is creating chaos
with more tariffs on China, with income tax fraud,
with the obstruction of justice, etc., etc., there's a hundred dairy cows
stopping all cars on this Moveen road as they cross
over to graze on rolling green hills.

Though countries and companies ravage our air and use broad
and false science to justify their actions,
there's a brown donkey behind this cottage
who stares at me with kindness, I think, and would applaud,
if he could, when I feed him an apple.

Though there are wars, death and suffering, people who run
for their lives, carrying children and clothes,
mothers and fathers blown to pieces, sorrow sinking into the earth,
I can walk to the edge of a cliff in Kilkee, stunned
by sight and sound, and swear there must be a God

who knows everything we can't know.
And though my heart breaks whenever I imagine my children
and grandchildren living beyond me after the final sickness,
I remember you, this soft touch of your lips, your body aglow
next to mine, the look in your eyes saying, *Sleep, love, sleep.*

IT'S WHAT YOU DO

There are more changes each time I return.
—Eilean Ni Chuilleanain, "Night Journeys"

This is the fifth rain today
and it's 2:31 in the afternoon. In between downpours, I've been
on a long walk in the sun, fed the asses in the back forty.

But now, it's raining again. People here,
mostly Catholic, if anything, seem pretty Zen
about the weather. Turn around three times fast
and the sky opens, wind rushes in off the bay
of Shannon. If it rains,
you put on a raincoat, grab an umbrella and live your life.
What's the alternative? Sulk inside and pray?
Let the world stumble forward while you go insane?

Rain or shine, cloudy or clear, windy or still,
the minutes click on. So get off your butt,
open the door and face whatever is thrown at you.

If you're out, laughing and singing, you'll forget each step
from this point
                    is downhill.

MY, HOW TIME CHANGES

When I had curls
I knew more girls.
I do more reading
now my hair is receding.

—James Simmons, "Epigrams"

My grandsons, three and four years old, beat me
at peeing every time, and it doesn't matter when
I start. They take great pleasure in this.

I used to be a decent basketball player,
but now with bad knees, I can't jump or run. I pretend
to understand the mechanic who tells me
my slip yoke and transmission solenoid should be replaced.
I hand over my wallet and smile.

After forty years of marriage, I still have no idea
what my wife is thinking, and I never will.

I push my body like a shopping cart down the aisle,
delaying the checkout while I can, wandering all over
this lovely place.

IT'S NOT WHAT YOU THINK

> *Where we live no longer matters*
> *If it ever did . . .*
> —Harry Clifton, "Where We Live"

And where we die, where we give up the last
bit of light burning in our soul
is forgettable
and useless. Once we're gone, we're gone for good, or bad,
or in truth, we become the mystery of what's beyond the hole
or the fire. Some say we climb on that ancient ship, raise the mast
and sail into heaven. Or perhaps we transform and come back
to earth as a robin, a squirrel, a yellow moth.
Maybe our soul
floats in the wind, blown around the world. Could nothing happen?
Maybe our bones and bone dust mix, turn into the ground-broth
that feeds the trees and plants, the corn and wheat in silos, stacked.

No, it's where we live and love and work to make ends meet
that matters down here. Who we hold and kiss,
who depends
on us, who cooks and eats with us, who lifts a glass or a prayer
in our name is what matters. A man's wish list
could be a mile long, a thousand items on huge sheets,
and it'd be worthless without love. A woman's dreams
may be honorable and gracious and sincere
but without love,
they'll shrivel on the vine of intention. It's not where you live and die,
but who you live and die with, who you love and hold dear,
and all the kind and decent things you do in between.

BLACK PLAGUE

—for Thomas Lynch

> *I cannot hear you over all the noise*
> *in both our lives.*
>
> —Sara Berkeley, "First Faun"

There's a tree in Carrigaholt
across from The Long Dock
with eleven crows' nests. It's hard to imagine
a tender crow mother, bringing bits of bread
and seed, cleaning feathers and filth from her tiny flock.

As crows land in the tree, it sounds like a revolt,
that brash cawing echoing across the bay
as baby birds cry out, *Look at me! Look at me!*
I can't help but think of Poe and Hitchcock
as I leave Carmody's pub, wondering if I'll make it to the car,
if they'll poke my eyes out or carry me away to sea.

If the birds came for me, what would I say?
Black is my favorite color? Here, take all my change?
No, I'd stand tall, let my eyes go gray
and tell them I know each egg is a poem
and each poem is a small crow who caws in the back
of my brain. In the pitch black sky, he glides and sways,
conjuring how and when to get his revenge.

IN YOUR SPARE TIME

> *I'm out in the garage, throwing mannequins*
> *around . . .*
>
> —Matthew Sweeney, "Iceland"

It's therapy
for the weak. Place five or six mannequins
in the garage, close the door
and beat the shit out of them when you're bored,
angry, frustrated, when you're drunk
and afraid to make a scene at Carmody's or O'Mara's.

You can dress the mannequins—this one, a tattooed punk,
that, a farmer. Here's a lady from the bank
who refuses to give you a loan. Your father, a bully, a garda.
Then wail away, tossing one across the room into the stone wall,
punching one up to the ceiling,
kicking and screaming until you're tired and sweaty,
nearly sober.

Now, go into the house, lie on the couch and catch your breath.
Confess to the psychiatrist mannequin sitting in the big chair
by the fire. List your grievances out loud, but in a quiet voice,
your wood's voice.
Once satisfied, carry the psychiatrist out to the garage
for tomorrow's battle.

Walking back to the house, stare up
into a sky with ten million stars and wave.
Your heart skips a beat
when you hear your wife, a blow-up doll,
calling you
from the bedroom.

THE ? ACT

The straw rope has turned into real gold.
—Michael Longley, "The Necklace"

From a blank canvas, one stroke of red paint

starts a sunset. Two hands on a piano
and a symphony is born.
This ball of wet clay spins, caressed
in someone's palms and rises like a torso
into a vase. It doesn't matter—a criminal or a saint,

a waitress or cop, a nurse, banker, farmer, child—
the urge to create burns in the blood.
With this piece of string, he says, I'll fashion
a beautiful woman. With this fabric and these candy wrappers,
she says, I'll build an ark for the flood.

My hand crawls across white paper, sometimes weeping,
sometimes wild.

OUT WITH A BANG

Who wouldn't want to fade out
in a blaze of glory?
—Dennis O'Driscoll, "Tulipomania"

Explain how to do this, exactly, from a hospital bed
with two tubes stuck in one arm and a heart monitor
beeping away. When you can't stand by yourself without a walker

and your feet won't listen to your brain, how do you start the blaze?
How do you bust out in glory? You can't even reach the front door
when the bell rings. Hell, it's difficult to lather the bread
for your peanut butter sandwich. So explain, please,
how you'd generate enough energy to explode
at the end, fireworks and streamers, music blaring
under the loud bangs and booms rocking through your ears.

You want the bright lights and sparkle. You want to speed
down the road, outrun the sirens, jump the river
and rise up, wiping stars from your sleeves.

BECOMING A FIDDLER

> *My last things will be first things slipping from me.*
> —Seamus Heaney, "Mint"

We've taken it on as our job to watch the sunset
                                every night.

We check the sunset times and drive out
to Diamond Rock for a grand view of ocean, waves and clouds
                                 in pink light
until the sun drowns in the horizon. It's hard to get
any better than this—on holiday in Ireland with my wife.
                                 After forty-one
years, we've discovered, luckily, we still like and love each other.

When we were younger, we planned out our tomorrows, couldn't wait
                                 for the sun
to rise. Today, we let the hours roll over us, watch the day disappear
                                 from sight.

A THIN SPACE

But a love poet must somehow make love
if only to language...
—Dennis O'Driscoll, "To a Love Poet"

I'm having a moment, you say

as we sit at a table by the ocean,
just us two on holiday for forty-one days,
the same number as our years
of marriage. There's Guinness, hot tea, sun
on your back, and it's the first Friday

out of six abroad. I love your moments,
filled to the brim and beyond with gratitude,
maybe joy, something divine and unexplainable.
You tear up, so I tear up—it just happens
after living so long together. Your mood
becomes my mood, my heart content

to be near your heart. Even if there's nothing
after the great darkness,
I'll swim to you, dig for you,
fly or jump or move stars to find you.
Of course, if there's a heaven and we're blessed,

I'll have a moment when I die and hear you begin to sing.

DOES POETRY PAY?

you have nothing
but the light of the penurious moon.
—Rita Ann Higgins, "Poetry Doesn't Pay"

Does faith pay enough to keep
the lights on in the apartment? Does hope
put gasoline in your car's tank?
Will dreams save the family farm
from bankruptcy? Even the pope
has bills to pay in order to keep
the chapels heated, food on the marble tables.

Will love open the skies and give you
the answer you deserve? If you forgive
yourself, will you be able to buy that Saab
or make a down payment on a new
house? Sorry, no. The moon rises above you.

It pushes and pulls.

A LOOP HEAD BLESSING

Another minute of innocence and rest.
—Dennis O'Driscoll, "3 AM"

I wake early and sneak out of bed

to wash, take my pills,
make coffee. I sit and read in the quiet.
This window, a vine covered turf shed,

that one, cows lumbering up the trail
under a cloudy sky over the hill
to a new pasture.
No rain so far, but it comes and goes

as it pleases. There's a chill
in the wind, uncommon on this scale
for late May. The whiff of manure
is sporadic but certain. Tonight, we're off to Doolin

for music and friends and a few lovely pints.
There's something simple and pure
about Nora's cottage—maybe the hay bales
in the fields, the three asses, the wild fuchsia, the imaginary grin

of the horses when the carrots come out.
If you sit here long enough, away from your normal life
and listen to your heart singing, the thin

place will open to a kind of heaven, brilliant and frail.

TELL ME WHAT I WANT TO HEAR

I'd love to squeeze your old bony hand for details.
—John Ennis, "Questions for W.C. Williams"

Wouldn't it be easier if we could just ask you, Lord,
for the answer? If I marry this girl, will we be fulfilled and happy?
Should I be a farmer,
a teacher, a mason, a priest?
How many children should we have? Will my name be on the marquee
in bright lights? Do I sell the ranch? Can I really afford

    to buy that cabin on the lake? The answers would flow like milk

and honey, drowning us in certainty. Maybe, though, we need to search
by ourselves, stand tall in the rain
and cry out to a silent god. Maybe
we need to wrestle our own demons and build a church
of wonder where we can kneel and forgive
our own guilt.

A FORK IN THE ROAD

As if to music, as if to peace.
—Eavan Boland, "Irish Poetry"

At the kitchen table with the sun reaching
in over the sink,
my lover for all these years
sleeping in the bedroom, I sip a cup of coffee

and save the world again. It's what poets do,
at least, in our minds. The man tries to cut off his ear
and we sew it back on. The woman has too much to drink,

downs a bottle of sleeping pills and we pump her stomach.
We lift, turn, hammer, carry, fix, massage, set
the world right. Anything and everything is possible

during these moments.
Like God, we can grab the boy by his hand or let

him fall; we can push the knife into the girl or
kiss her moonlit neck.

THE LONG FALL

Let no love poem ever come to this threshold.
—Eavan Boland, "Quarantine"

Right to the edge of the cliff
on the loop head south of Kilkee,
there's a four-hundred foot drop into jagged rock.

I stand on the cushiony grass,
staring down at crashing waves below,
the rippling hulk of the Atlantic
churning into itself, then letting go,
sound of water crushing into rock and water.

Would I fall from this threshold
to prove my heart's desire?
Would I leap off into oblivion
to save your life?   May love find
                the faith to step away from the edge
                    and walk back into town with us,
                        singing to the yellow moon.

GRAVITY'S RULE

. . . while time bends you slowly
back to the ground.
—John Montague, "To Cease"

There's an actual candelabra at Nora's cottage
tied to a dolly that allows you
to lower it, light the six candles and lift it back up,
left over from before electricity, I'd wager.

Since it's been warm this spring,
the heat has bent two,
maybe three candles into nearly horizontal positions.
I'll have to lower it and replace them
before we leave, but we're here through
mid-June. Still have twenty days
to enjoy the metaphor—how we're all undone
over time, leaning into the earth.

What I wouldn't give to tack on thirty
or forty good years. Hell, I'd promise to be stunned
by every sunrise, sunset. Hell, I'd promise, every day,
                to sing.

IT STARTS WITH G, LIKE GOD

—for John Woods

Your ashes will not stir, even on this high ground ...
—Derek Mahon, "In Carrowdore Cemetery"

This time, Virginia Beach, May 31st, twelve people killed.
Tomorrow, it could be at your grocery store,

your workplace, your favorite bar, a gas station.
Next week, it could happen on your street as you grill
hot dogs and red onions. This is not normal or sane.

And where's the turning point? How many more
have to die senselessly, kids, parents, employees,

before something is done to keep guns
out of certain people's hands? I'm bored
with prayers and words of compassion. I'm sick

of vague platitudes and political apathy.
There is no justification possible that includes the bloody murder

of innocents. It's time. It's beyond time. As the funerals wind down,
the nightmares begin, the curses and regrets and pleas.
We all dress and go out, a bulls-eye on our backs,

ready for someone's aim.

THE BIG ROOM

The room was loud with noise of dying men.
Brendan Kennelly, "At the Party"

That's any room, and not just men, but dying
                women, dying boys and girls. The world coughs
                        and seven animals go extinct.
We have to sit up and take notice, hell,
take action if we're going to save even half
                of the million endangered species. Why is it as we're trying
to find ourselves and how to be happy,
                        we end up killing animals, ruining the air
                        and water, ripping wide the ozone layer?

I'd love to live a day and be completely harmless.
I'd love to live in a way that removes despair
                from someone's life, that gives a family hope, that feeds a baby.
It's true, there's a room,
                        it's noisy, everyone's dying in it, and we all stand there
                        with a choice to make: we can stuff our ears, close our eyes,
and do whatever the hell we want,

or we can live gently, think of others, share
                        our good fortune and work to make sure tomorrow rises
                        with a smile and blooms.

A WOMAN DRESSES, A MAN WATCHES

When a terrible truth
strikes and your heart cries out, being carried off...
—Eamon Greanan, "Detail"

Someone is always sleeping. Someone
is always drinking. One plows a field, another dies,
this one swims alone, that one cooks a meal over an open fire.

A woman dresses in a white gown. A man watches a boat drift
out on the sea. The waves roll into shore; the tide
comes in and goes out. A quilt is finished; a song is begun.

If there's a meaning or order or design to this
world, no one living can say for sure.
We guess, believe, surmise, wonder and question,
but we're like pigs in a mud pit, rooting around for stars.

Some say there's a divine plan; others claim it's a mystery, an absurd
play. All we really know is someone's heart is breaking,
                    someone else is being kissed.

BLUEPRINT

. . . you built this house in me.
—Enda Wyley, "The House"

From the ground up,

you set the corners, nailed the frame,
laid a foundation
that's stood over forty years so far
and will go the distance all the same.
                    You're my full plate and cup
of wine, my open door,
my garden, my tree, my heart.
                    When it rains, you have a room

in me; when it snows, you have a bed here
to lie down. I'll carry in more peat
for the fire and cut another cord
of wood, if needed, to keep you warm.
                    So set your bags down, rest your bones,
close your eyes and dream away your worries.
You built this house, love,
hand placing every brick and stone.

Now it's time to come in from the storm.

ABOUT THE AUTHOR

photo: Debra James

David James lives in a two-light town in mid-Michigan with his wife of forty-three years. Blessed to have three children and six grandchildren, he teaches writing for Oakland Community College. James has published five full-length books, six chapbooks, and has had over thirty of his one-act plays produced in the U.S. and Ireland.

www.ingramcontent.com/pod-product-compliance
Lightning Source LLC
LaVergne TN
LVHW051801080426
835511LV00018B/3375